THE

PROPHET'S

DIET

A Lifestyle According To Yeshua's Design.

I0155482

AUDREA V. HEARD

© 2024
IBG Publications, Inc.
www.ibgpublications.com

AUDREA V. HEARD

Published by I.B.G. Publications, Inc., a Power to Wealth Company

Web Address: WWW.IBGPublications.Com

admin@IBGPublications.Com / 904-419-9810

Copyright, 2022 by Audrea V. Abraham

IBG Publications, Inc., Orange Park, FL

ISBN: 978-1-956266-74-0

Heard, Audrea V.

The Prophet's Diet: A Lifestyle According To Yeshua's Design

Printed in the United States of America.

DEDICATION

This book is dedicated to young and old prophets who represent the kingdom of the Most High.

The prophet is a peculiar being in the kingdom of God, and one must be willing and ready to answer the call. Answering the call will also mean living a strict lifestyle to purify the prophetic gift.

This book is your prophetic guide on how to live and maintain a lifestyle according to Yeshua's design. Get ready to take your assignment to the next dimension!

AUDREA V. HEARD

TABLE OF CONTENTS

CHAPTER 7:

ACKNOWLEDGMENTS

I acknowledge the Holy Spirit, who has been my guide in the prophetic realm for over 20 years. Without Your sharpening and on-the-job training, I would not be a tool for the Master's use.

For many years, I searched for a mentor in the earthly realm, often overlooking Your presence. When I finally embraced and surrendered to Your tutelage, my spiritual walk was transformed.

As I continue my journey into eternity, I give You free reign to lead and guide me into all truth (John 16:13).

DISCLAIMER

The author has made every attempt to provide information that is accurate and complete, but this book is not intended as a substitute for professional, medical advice. This book is not meant to be used, nor should it be used, to diagnose or treat any medical or psychological condition.

DIET:

-food and drink considered in terms of its qualities, composition, and its effects on health.

-a particular selection of food, especially as designed or prescribed to improve a person's physical condition or to prevent   or treat a disease.

-anything that is habitually provided or partaken of.

-https://dictionary.com

LIFESTYLE:

-the habits, attitudes, tastes, moral standards, economic level, etc., that together constitute the mode of living of an individual or group.

-https://dictionary.com

*H*ebrew *T*reasure

"Prophets should
not only instruct others
on how to live but also
embody the first fruits of a
close relationship   with the
Most High, demonstrating
the benefits through
their own lives."

— *A*postle *A*udrea *V*. *A*braham

INTRODUCTION

I decided to write this book to give prophets a guideline upon which to live their everyday life. I have become grieved in my spirit when I see overweight, fat preachers and ESECIALLY prophets.

A man/woman who has no rule over what they put in their mouth is most likely a person who does not have the discipline to spend hours on end in the presence of the Most High. There is just no way you can pray for hours on end or perform deliverance through an unhealthy temple.

It was the year 2016 when the Most High gave me instructions on how to live my life with food and other products we use daily. I began to uncover truths about the body that did not necessarily come from the Bible, but from research and further study.

I am a prophet who was born and raised in the West, a place where having physical and spiritual discipline is highly lacking. It was after being led by the Holy Spirit that I gave up meat, dairy and other products. To say it was a challenge is an understatement. It was by far the most challenging thing I ever did. But through His grace and mercy, I was overcome by the blood of the lamb and by the word of my testimony.

In 2022, I relapsed. I say 'relapsed' because not only did I return to meat, but I was back eating sugar, junk and other comfort foods. It was about a year of spiraling out of control when I came to the realization that rejecting the 'king's meat' was the way the Most High had chosen for me to live.

People would often ask me, "WHY did you give up meat?' Consistently, my response was, "The Holy Spirit told me to."

And as sure as He told me to give it up in 2016, He has instructed me to return to this way of living in

2023 after my relapse. I struggled for many months with this decision. But as of the time of this writing, I am back in full swing with the lifestyle I know works for my health (most importantly) and secondly to sharpen the prophetic seed living inside me.

As we journey through this book, I am going to share research on the lifestyle of a prophet, its benefits and the simplest ways to hear or see with your prophetic gift. Please take what I am saying as a guide, and not the final say about how you should live your life as a prophet. Each person has his/her own individual, unique calling from he Most High, and it requires a different set of rules for each one of us.

This book serves as a foundation as you seek Him further on how He desires *you* to live. But keep in mind, He has a path ordained for YOU. The main point of this writing is to ignite you to live in your prophetic truth the way HE designed.

Significance Of Biblical Prophets

The Bible, a timeless spiritual and historical text, is replete with stories of faith, miracles, and divine guidance. Among its many narratives, the lives of the prophets stand out as exemplary models of devotion, obedience, and profound connection with God.

These men and women, chosen to deliver God's messages to His people, often led lives marked by extraordinary circumstances and rigorous spiritual disciplines. One intriguing aspect of their lives that frequently intersects with their prophetic missions is their diet.

The diets of Biblical prophets are more than mere details of their daily lives; they are imbued with rich symbolism, divine instruction, and profound spiritual lessons. From Elijah's miraculous sustenance by ravens during a severe drought to Daniel's steadfast refusal of the king's lavish food, the dietary choices of these prophets provide a unique lens through which we can understand their unwavering faith and commitment.

These narratives offer insights not only into the historical and cultural contexts of ancient Israel but also into the spiritual principles that guided these remarkable individuals in the New Testament.

This book embarks on a journey to explore the diets of Biblical prophets, delving into the significance of their food choices and the spiritual messages they convey.

We will examine the specific dietary practices of notable prophets such as Elijah, Daniel, Ezekiel, John the Baptist, Jesus Christ and other New Testament prophets, uncovering the deeper meanings behind their sustenance. Through their stories, we will see how their diets reflect their dependence on God, their obedience to His commands, and their dedication to living lives set apart for divine purposes.

Moreover, we will draw parallels between the dietary practices of the prophets and the teachings of the New Testament. Jesus Christ, often referred to as the greatest prophet, and the Apostle Paul, one of the most influential early Christian leaders, both provided transformative teachings on food and dietary laws. Their perspectives will help us understand the evolution of these practices and their relevance to contemporary faith.

In exploring the diets of Biblical prophets, this book aims to provide readers with a deeper appreciation of the spiritual lessons embedded in these ancient narratives. Whether you are a scholar of religious texts, a devout believer seeking to enrich your faith, or simply curious about the intersection of food and spirituality, this book offers valuable insights into the profound connections between what we eat and how we live out our faith.

Join us as we delve into the fascinating world of the prophets' diets, uncovering the timeless wisdom and spiritual nourishment that these Biblical accounts continue to offer today.

*H*ebrew *T*reasure

What is the Torah?

-The Torah is the compilation of the first five books of the Hebrew Bible, namely the books of Genesis, Exodus, Leviticus, Numbers and Deuteronomy.

-**https://en.wikipedia.org/wiki/Torah**

CHAPTER I:

Dietary Practices In Ancient Israel

Dietary practices in ancient Israel were deeply intertwined with cultural, religious, and social values, reflecting a profound connection between faith and daily life. The dietary laws and customs outlined in the Torah provided a framework not only for what could be eaten but also for how food was to be prepared, consumed, and enjoyed. These practices were more than just guidelines for nourishment; they were expressions of spiritual devotion, community identity, and adherence to divine commandments.

Central to these practices were the kosher laws, which dictated permissible and forbidden foods and established guidelines for their preparation. These laws reinforced the distinctiveness of the Israelite community and their covenant with God.

The everyday diet of ancient Israelites included a variety of foods such as bread, fruits, vegetables, and meats, all of which played significant roles in their cultural and religious rituals.

Food also held considerable symbolic and ritual significance. Festivals and religious observances were marked by specific meals and offerings, each imbued with meaning and tradition. From the Passover Seder, which commemorates liberation from Egypt to the Sabbath meals that celebrate rest and reflection, food was integral to religious practice and communal life.

Understanding these dietary practices provides insight into the holistic nature of ancient Israelite spirituality, where every meal was an opportunity to honor God, connect with community, and express identity.

This next section delves into the kosher laws, common foods, and the rich cultural and religious significance of food in ancient Israel.

A. General Food Customs and Laws

1. *Kosher Laws:*

- **Definition**: The term "kosher" refers to food that complies with Jewish dietary laws, known as "kashrut." These laws are outlined in the Torah and include both ethical and ritual requirements.

- **Permissible Animals**: Only animals that both chew their cud and have split hooves are considered kosher (e.g., cows, sheep). Pigs and camels are not kosher.
- **Seafood**: Only fish with fins and scales are kosher (e.g., tuna, salmon). Shellfish and other sea creatures are not permitted.
- **Birds**: Specific birds are considered kosher, excluding birds of prey.
- **Slaughtering**: Animals must be slaughtered in a humane manner (shechita) by a trained individual (shochet), ensuring minimal suffering.
- **Separation of Meat and Dairy**: Meat and dairy products must be prepared and consumed separately. This extends to utensils and cookware, which should be designated for either meat or dairy.

2. *Common Foods and Meals:*

- **Bread and Grains**: Bread, particularly unleavened bread (matzah) during Passover, was a staple. Other grains like barley and wheat were also common.
- **Fruits and Vegetables**: Commonly consumed fruits included grapes, figs, dates, and olives. Vegetables like onions, garlic, and leeks were prevalent.

- **Meat and Fish**: Meat from kosher animals was a significant part of festive meals, while fish was commonly eaten, provided it met kosher standards.
- **Legumes and Nuts**: Lentils, beans, and various nuts were included in the diet.
- **Wine and Oil**: Wine was a staple beverage, especially during religious ceremonies. Olive oil was used for cooking and anointing.

B. Cultural and Religious Significance of Food

I. Symbolism:

- **Blessings and Thanksgiving**: Food was often associated with blessings and thanksgiving to God. Meals were opportunities to express gratitude and recognize God's provision.
- **Sacrifices and Offerings**: Certain foods, particularly those used in offerings and sacrifices (e.g., the burnt offering, peace offering), held significant religious meaning. These offerings symbolized devotion and were integral to worship practices.

II. Festivals and Rituals:

- **Passover**: Celebrated with unleavened bread (matzah) to commemorate the Exodus from

Egypt. The meal (Seder) includes symbolic foods such as bitter herbs and charoset.

- **Sukkot**: The Feast of Tabernacles involved meals in temporary booths, highlighting the time Israelites spent in the wilderness.
- **Shabbat**: The Sabbath meal, including challah bread and wine, marked the weekly day of rest and spiritual reflection.

III. Health and Hygiene:

- **Dietary Laws for Health**: Some dietary restrictions, such as the prohibition of consuming certain unclean animals, also had practical health benefits, potentially reducing exposure to diseases and parasites.
- **Cleanliness and Purity**: Food preparation and consumption practices were deeply intertwined with concepts of ritual purity, emphasizing spiritual cleanliness and adherence to God's commands.

IV. Kosher Laws (Kashrut)

1. **Definition and significance**: Kosher laws are dietary guidelines derived from the Torah, particularly in Leviticus and Deuteronomy, dictating what foods are permissible (kosher) and forbidden (non-kosher) for consumption.

Clean and unclean animals:

- **Land animals**: Only animals that chew the cud and have cloven hooves are permitted (e.g., cattle, sheep, goats). Forbidden animals include pigs and camels.
- **Seafood**: Only fish with fins and scales are allowed. Shellfish and other non-scaled fish are prohibited.
- **Birds**: Permissible birds are not explicitly listed, but birds of prey and scavengers are forbidden.
- **Insects**: Generally prohibited, except for specific locusts, crickets, and grasshoppers.
- **Slaughtering practices**: Animals must be slaughtered in a specific manner (shechita) to be considered kosher. This involves a swift, humane cut to the throat, ensuring minimal suffering and proper blood drainage.
- **Separation of meat and dairy**: Meat and dairy products cannot be consumed together. Separate utensils, dishes, and preparation areas are required to prevent cross-contamination.

V. *Common Foods and Meals*

- **Grains**: Barley, wheat, spelt, oats, and rye were staple foods, often prepared as bread, porridge, or gruel.

- **Fruits and vegetables**: Olives, figs, dates, pomegranates, grapes, cucumbers, leeks, onions, garlic, and various legumes were commonly consumed.
- **Meat and fish**: Meat was less commonly eaten due to its expense but included lamb, goat, and beef. Fish from the Mediterranean Sea and the Sea of Galilee were also part of the diet.
- **Dairy**: Milk, cheese, and yogurt from goats and sheep were commonly consumed.
- **Seasonings and Sweeteners**: Salt, herbs, and honey were used to flavor food. Olive oil was a primary fat for cooking and dressing.
- **Beverages**: Water, wine, and occasionally milk were the primary drinks. Wine was often diluted with water.

VI. *Cultural and Religious Significance of Food*

- **Festivals and sacrifices**: Certain foods were central to religious festivals (e.g., unleavened bread during Passover) and sacrificial rituals in the Temple.
- **Sabbath meals**: Special meals were prepared for the Sabbath, including challah (braided bread) and wine.
- **Food as a symbol of hospitality**: Offering food to guests was a key aspect of hospitality and social interaction.

o **Fasting and feasting**: Periods of fasting (e.g., Yom Kippur) and feasting (e.g., Sukkot) were integral to religious observance, with specific dietary practices associated with each.

This section provides a comprehensive overview of the dietary practices and customs in ancient Israel, highlighting the significance of kosher laws and common foods in daily life and religious observance.

If you have done enough extensive research and study, you would know if you have Hebrew roots, and this is not an extinct people on the face of the Earth.

This brief look at dietary laws in ancient Israel is meant to serve as the foundation that we should live by whether a Jew, prophet or not.

CHAPTER 2:

Specific Prophets & Their Diets

The dietary practices of prophets in ancient Israel offer a unique glimpse into the intersection of spiritual vocation and daily sustenance.

These men and women, chosen by God to deliver His messages and lead His people, often followed distinctive dietary habits that reflected their spiritual journeys and divine mandates. By examining the diets of specific prophets—such as Elijah, Elisha, and Daniel—we gain valuable insights into how their food choices were intertwined with their prophetic missions and experiences.

These diets were not merely about nourishment but were deeply symbolic, illustrating themes of reliance on God, obedience to divine instructions, and the physical and spiritual challenges faced during their prophetic callings. This chapter explores the dietary practices of notable prophets, highlighting how their eating habits were a manifestation of their faith and service.

OLD TESTAMENT PROPHETS

The Old Testament prophets were pivotal figures in the spiritual and social life of ancient Israel, serving as God's messengers and leaders during times of both crisis and renewal. Their lives were marked by profound dedication, often involving unique and symbolic practices that set them apart from others.

One aspect of their distinct lifestyle was their diet, which not only sustained them physically but also carried significant spiritual and symbolic meaning.

From Elijah's sustenance provided by ravens to Daniel's adherence to a diet of vegetables and water, the dietary habits of these prophets reflected their obedience to divine commands and their reliance on God's provision.

This chapter will explore how the diets of Old Testament prophets were deeply connected to their prophetic roles and missions, offering insights into their unwavering faith and commitment.

Let's take a closer look at a few of the Old Testament

prophets and their diets.

A. Elijah

1. **Diet during the drought (1 Kings 17:2-6)**.
   a. Ravens bring bread and meat.
   b. Elijah was provided with bread and meat by ravens, as instructed by God. This miraculous provision sustained him during a time of severe drought and famine.
   c. This diet proved the supernatural provision of the Most High. This proved as a time when Elijah had to trust Him for every meal.

2. **Drinking from the brook**
   a. Elijah drank water from the brook Cherith, which later dried up due to the ongoing drought.
   b. The Most High was aware of his need for water, so he provided this brook to sustain him. This term is often used in sermons to describe the supernatural river of the living God.

3. **Diet provided by the widow of Zarephath (1 Kings 17:8-16)**
   a. Flour and oil for bread.
   b. Elijah was sustained by a widow in Zarephath who only had a handful of flour and a little oil. Through Elijah's prophetic promise, the flour and oil

miraculously did not run out until the drought ended.

B. Daniel

1. **Refusal of the king's food (Daniel 1:8-16).**
   a. Preference for vegetables and water.
   b. Daniel and his companions refused the rich food and wine from the king's table, choosing instead to eat vegetables and drink water.
2. **Resulting in health and strength.**
   a. Despite their simple diet, Daniel and his friends appeared healthier and stronger than those who ate the king's food.
3. **Impact of dietary choices on his faith and leadership.**
   a. Daniel's dietary choices were a statement of his faith and commitment to God's laws, leading to God's favor and his rise to a position of influence in the Babylonian court.

C. Ezekiel

1. **Symbolic diet (Ezekiel 4:9-17).**
2. **Recipe for bread.**
   a. God instructed Ezekiel to make bread from a mix of grains, including

wheat, barley, beans, lentils, millet, and spelt.

3. **Cooking over cow dung.**
   a. Originally instructed to cook the bread over human dung as a symbol of defilement, Ezekiel persuaded God to allow him to use cow dung instead (**Ezekiel 4:10-15**).

4. **Symbolism of scarcity and suffering.**
   a. This diet symbolized the scarcity and suffering that would come upon Jerusalem during the siege.

COMPARISON WITH NEW TESTAMENT TEACHINGS

The prophets of the New Testament, while continuing the tradition of divine communication established in the Old Testament, represent a shift in the prophetic landscape marked by the advent of Christ and the early Christian church.

Unlike their Old Testament predecessors, who often operated within the context of Israel's national identity and covenant with God, New Testament prophets emerged in a rapidly expanding, diverse, and sometimes hostile environment. These prophets, such as John the Baptist and the apostles, not only foretold future events but also provided guidance and encouragement to nascent Christian communities.

While Old Testament prophets like Elijah and Isaiah were often solitary figures challenging kings and nations, New Testament prophets worked within a communal framework, emphasizing the fulfillment of prophecy through Christ and the spread of the gospel.

This section explores these continuities and contrasts, illuminating how the role and influence of prophets evolved from the Old to the New Testament eras.

NEW TESTAMENT PROPHETS

In the New Testament, several individuals are recognized as prophets or are noted for their prophetic gifts.

Here are some key figures:

A. John the Baptist
Role: John the Baptist is considered a prophet who prepared the way for Jesus Christ.

Key Passages: Matthew 3:1-12, Mark 1:2-8, Luke 3:1-18, John 1:19-34

The diet of John the Baptist:

1. *Diet in the wilderness* (Matthew 3:4, Mark 1:6):
   a. Locusts and wild honey

    b. John the Baptist's diet consisted of locusts and wild honey, reflecting his ascetic lifestyle and separation from worldly comforts.

2. *Ascetic lifestyle and its significance:*
    a. His simple diet and lifestyle underscored his prophetic mission of calling people to repentance and preparation for the coming of the Messiah.

B. Jesus Christ

Role: Jesus is not only the Messiah, but He is also acknowledged as a prophet by the people of His time.

Key Passages: Matthew 21:11, Luke 7:16, John 4:19

Jesus' perspective on food and dietary laws:

1. Teachings on clean and unclean foods (**Mark 7:14-23**).
2. Miracles involving food (e.g., feeding the 5000; **Matthew 14:13-21**).
3. Freedom in Christ regarding food (**Romans 14, 1 Corinthians 8**).

C. Agabus

Role: Agabus is a prophet mentioned in the Acts of the Apostles who made specific predictions about future events.

Key Passages: Acts 11:27-28 (predicts a famine), Acts 21:10-11 (predicts Paul's imprisonment)

D. Anna

Role: Anna was a prophetess who recognized Jesus as the Messiah when He was presented at the temple.

Key Passages: Luke 2:36-38

Lifestyle Of Anna:

According to the passage of scripture in the book of Luke, Anna was known to give herself wholly to fasting and prayers. We know that fasting is *abstinence* of food.

E. Philip's Daughters

Role: Philip the Evangelist had four unmarried daughters who prophesied.

Key Passages: Acts 21:9

Role: Other prophets and prophetic gifts in the early church-the New Testament references other prophets and individuals with prophetic gifts within the early Christian communities.

Key Passages:

Acts 13:1: Mentions prophets and teachers in the church at Antioch, including Barnabas, Simeon, Lucius, Manaen, and Saul (Paul).

1 Corinthians 12:28-29: Paul lists prophets as one of the spiritual gifts within the church.

Ephesians 4:11: Paul mentions prophets as part of the five-fold ministry gifts given to the church.

Prophetic Encouragement and Warnings

Role: Prophets in the New Testament often provided guidance, encouragement, and warnings to the early church.

Key Passages:

1 Corinthians 14:1-5: Paul encourages the church to desire the gift of prophecy for the edification of the church.

1 Thessalonians 5:20: Paul advises the church not to despise prophecies but to test everything.

These individuals and passages highlight the continuation and importance of prophetic ministry in the New Testament era, building on the rich tradition of Old Testament prophecy.

New Testament Diets & Dietary Law:

While the New Testament does not explicitly list the diet and dietary laws of most of its prophets (save John the Baptist), it is safe to assume that they took on the dietary laws of ancient Israel, while more liberty was provided through Jesus Christ. We can say with confidence that they maintained lifestyles of fasting and praying.

General insights can be drawn from the cultural and historical context of the time, as well as specific references to certain individuals.

General Diet Of People In The New Testament Era

In the time of the New Testament, the diet of people in the Mediterranean region, including Israel, would have been based on locally available foods.

This typically included:

- **Grains**: Bread was a staple, often made from wheat or barley.

- **Legumes**: Lentils and beans were common.

- **Fruits**: Figs, grapes, pomegranates, and olives were widely consumed.

- **Vegetables**: Onions, garlic, leeks, and various greens.

- **Fish**: Fish was a significant part of the diet, especially for those living near bodies of water.

- **Meat**: Meat was less common but included lamb, goat, and occasionally beef, often reserved for special occasions or sacrifices.

- **Dairy**: Milk, cheese, and yogurt from goats and sheep.

- **Nuts and Seeds**: Almonds, pistachios, and other nuts.

- **Honey**: Used as a sweetener.

- **Wine**: Commonly consumed, often diluted with water.

Early Christian Community Practices

The early Christian community, including those with prophetic gifts, would have followed the dietary customs of their Jewish background, adhering to the kosher laws:

- **Clean vs. Unclean Foods**: They would have avoided foods considered unclean according to Levitical law (Leviticus 11).

- **Passover and Other Feasts**: Participation in Jewish feasts and festivals, which included specific dietary practices.

- **Breaking Bread**: Communal meals, often involving the breaking of bread and sharing of wine, which were central to early Christian gatherings (**Acts 2:42-47**).

While the New Testament does not provide extensive details about the diets of prophets or other figures, the general diet of people in the region, combined with specific references like John the Baptist's ascetic diet, provides a picture of the foods that would have been consumed by New Testament prophets and early Christians. The focus on simple, locally available, and culturally appropriate foods is evident.

<u>Symbolism and Lessons from Prophets' Diets</u>

Now, let's take some time to look at what these diets symbolize. Whenever prophets are instructed to eat a certain type of way, there was a reason for these instructions. It meant the Most High knew what was coming, their physical makeup and the minimum amount of food they could survive on. He created and engineered the human body, and He knows our most intricate details (**Psalm 139:14**).

A. Dependence on God for Sustenance:

- **<u>Elijah's Provision by Ravens</u>**: The miraculous provision of food by ravens for Elijah during the drought illustrates a complete reliance on God for survival. This act demonstrates that God can provide in the most unexpected ways and circumstances.

- **Elijah and the Widow of Zarephath**: The endless supply of flour and oil for Elijah, the widow, and her son highlights God's ability to sustain those who trust in Him, even in times of severe scarcity.

- **Daniel's Health and Strength**: Daniel's choice to eat only vegetables and drink water, coupled with his improved health, shows that God's sustenance transcends physical nourishment and is a testament to His provision and blessing on those who remain faithful.

B. *Symbolic Acts of Obedience and Prophecy:*

- **Ezekiel's Bread**: Ezekiel's consumption of bread made from various grains and cooked over cow dung served as a prophetic act symbolizing the impending famine and suffering Jerusalem would face. This act of obedience conveyed a powerful message to the Israelites about the consequences of their disobedience.

- **John the Baptist's Diet**: John the Baptist's diet of locusts and wild honey was a symbolic act of his prophetic role. It represented his separation from worldly indulgences and his dedication to preparing the way for Jesus.

C. *Lessons on Simplicity and Self-Denial:*

- **John the Baptist's Ascetic Lifestyle**: John's simple diet exemplifies the virtues of asceticism, self-denial, and focus on spiritual matters. His lifestyle encourages believers to prioritize spiritual growth over material comforts.
- **Daniel's Choice of Vegetables and Water**: Daniel's decision to abstain from the king's rich food and drink highlights the importance of self-control and the benefits of a simple diet. His example teaches the value of maintaining personal integrity and discipline in the face of external pressures.

D. Dietary Practices as Expressions of Faith and Commitment:

- **Daniel's Dietary Faithfulness**: Daniel's refusal to defile himself with the king's food was a profound expression of his faith and commitment to God's laws. This act of devotion set him apart and led to God's favor and blessings.
- **Ezekiel's Obedience**: Ezekiel's adherence to God's instructions regarding his diet, despite its unpalatability, underscores the importance of obedience in prophetic ministry. His actions were a tangible demonstration of his commitment to God's message and mission.
- **Elijah's Trust in God's Provision**: Elijah's reliance on God's provision during the drought illustrates a deep trust in God's faithfulness. His

diet, dictated by divine intervention, serves as a reminder of the importance of trusting God in all circumstances.

These symbolic acts and dietary practices not only provide insights into the lives of the prophets but also offer valuable lessons for contemporary believers on faith, obedience, simplicity, and reliance on God.

Comparison With New Testament Teachings

A. Jesus' Perspective on Food and Dietary Laws:

1. **Teachings on Clean and Unclean Foods (Mark 7:14-23)**

   - **Context**: Jesus challenges the Pharisees' and teachers of the law regarding their strict adherence to traditional dietary laws.
   - **Key Teaching**: Jesus declares that it is not what goes into a person that defiles them, but what comes out of their heart. This teaching shifts the focus from external dietary laws to the internal state of a person's heart and actions.
   - **Implications**: By emphasizing that all foods are clean, Jesus paves the way for a new understanding of purity and holiness that transcends dietary restrictions.

2. **Miracles Involving Food (e.g., Feeding the 5000)**

- **Feeding the 5000** (Matthew 14:13-21; Mark 6:30-44; Luke 9:10-17; John 6:1-14): Jesus miraculously multiplies five loaves of bread and two fish to feed a large crowd, demonstrating God's abundant provision.
- **Symbolism**: This miracle signifies Jesus as the Bread of Life, who provides spiritual nourishment and sustenance beyond physical food.

- **Teaching**: The miracle illustrates the importance of faith, gratitude, and the belief that God can provide for all needs.

B. Apostle Paul's Teachings on Food and Dietary Practices:

1. **Freedom in Christ Regarding Food (Romans 14, 1 Corinthians 8):**
   - *Romans 14:1-23*: Paul addresses disputes over dietary practices, emphasizing that believers should not judge one another over food choices. He encourages acceptance and understanding, highlighting that the kingdom of God is not about eating and drinking but about righteousness, peace, and joy in the Holy Spirit.

o *1 Corinthians 8:1-13*: Paul discusses the issue of eating food sacrificed to idols. He acknowledges that while believers have the freedom to eat anything, they should be mindful of the impact on others, particularly those with weaker consciences.

2. **Respecting Others' Dietary Choices.**

- ***Principle of Love and Edification***: Paul emphasizes that believers should prioritize the spiritual well-being of others over their own freedoms. If a particular food causes a fellow believer to stumble, it is better to abstain out of love and consideration.

- ***Unity and Harmony***: By respecting diverse dietary practices, believers foster unity and harmony within the Christian community. This approach encourages mutual respect and sensitivity to different cultural and spiritual backgrounds.

This comparison highlights the evolution of dietary practices from the Old Testament prophets to the New Testament teachings. Jesus and Paul both emphasize the importance of the internal state of faith and love over external dietary laws, promoting a more inclusive and spiritually focused approach to food and dietary practices.

AUDREA V. HEARD

CHAPTER 3:

Food's Effects On The Body & Pineal Gland

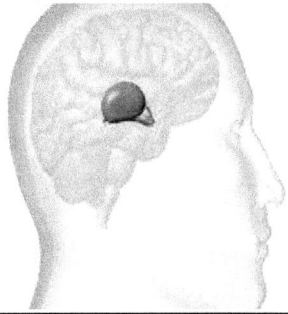

"The eye is the lamp of the body. If your eye is healthy, your whole body will be full of light"

~Matthew 6:22

The third eye/pineal gland is the place where God meets with us. It is also the door by which an individual can "see" into the spirit realm by way of spiritual gifts such as the discernment of spirits, quickening, words of knowledge, words of wisdom, dreams and so on.

Do you recall where I said I was born and raised in the introduction? If you remembered the west, then you are correct!

43

The problem with Western culture is that we have been so conditioned by the healthcare system that we, as believers, often fail to consult the Most High about what we should consume. We give the doctor's voice more weight than His, and as a result, we may end up dying before our time.

I understand you might think your doctor knows best. They have spent years studying, learning, and pondering how the human body works and functions. They leave medical school with all this 'knowledge,' yet they are still considered to be 'practicing' medicine. They are not the creator of the human body and will never know better than the Creator Himself how to treat it without consulting Him.

The Most High gave us the Levitical laws because He knew what would prolong life and nourish the temples He created.

The dietary habits prevalent in Western culture, characterized by a high consumption of processed foods, refined sugars, unhealthy fats, and large portion sizes, can have significant effects on the body, particularly for those in prophetic ministry.

For prophets, maintaining a healthy body is essential for their spiritual, mental, and physical well-being, as their role requires clarity, energy, and resilience.

Negative Effects

Here are the negative effects these things have on the body:

1. ***Processed Foods and Additives:***

   - **Health Issues**: High intake of processed foods can lead to various health problems, including obesity, diabetes, cardiovascular diseases, and digestive disorders. These conditions can hinder a prophet's *physical stamina* and overall well-being.
   - **Mental Clarity**: Artificial additives, preservatives, and high sugar content can affect mental clarity and cognitive function, which are crucial for receiving and interpreting divine messages.

2. ***Refined Sugars:***

   - **Energy Levels**: Consumption of refined sugars can cause spikes and crashes in blood sugar levels, leading to fluctuating energy levels and mood swings. Consistent energy is vital for the demanding nature of prophetic work.
   - **Inflammation**: Refined sugars contribute to inflammation in the body, which can

exacerbate chronic health issues and impair physical comfort and mobility.

3. *Unhealthy Fats:*

- **Heart Health**: Diets high in trans fats and saturated fats are linked to heart disease and other cardiovascular problems. A healthy heart is essential for maintaining physical endurance and vitality.

- **Brain Function**: Unhealthy fats can negatively impact brain health, affecting memory, focus, and emotional stability, all of which are important for a prophet's ministry.

4. *Large Portion Sizes:*

- **Overeating**: The tendency to consume large portions can lead to overeating and weight gain, which can affect physical agility and overall health.
- **Digestive Health**: Overeating can strain the digestive system, causing discomfort and affecting a prophet's ability to engage fully in their spiritual duties.

Positive Practices

A prophet should practice eating healthy and exercising on a regular basis, not just when it is time to use their gift. A prophet who maintains a healthy lifestyle is more likely to be ready when dispatched at a moment's notice by the Most High.

Here is a suggested eating regimen:

1. **_Whole Foods:_**

    • **Nutrient-Rich**: Incorporating more whole foods, such as fruits, vegetables, whole grains, and lean proteins, provides essential nutrients that support overall health, energy levels, and mental clarity.
    • **Natural State**: Foods in their natural state are free from harmful additives and preservatives, promoting better digestion and bodily function.

2. **_Balanced Diet_**:

    • **Macronutrients**: A balanced intake of carbohydrates, proteins, and fats ensures that the body receives the energy and nutrients needed for sustained physical and mental activity.

- **Micronutrients**: Vitamins and minerals from a varied diet support immune function, brain health, and emotional well-being.

3. *Hydration:*

- **Water Intake**: Adequate hydration is crucial for maintaining physical health, cognitive function, and energy levels. Drinking plenty of water helps detoxify the body and supports overall well-being.
- **Coconut Water**: Coconut water is an excellent source of electrolytes and helps to give the body what it needs to remain hydrated. This is a better choice over Gatorade and other drinks that may be high in sugar.

4. *Mindful Eating:*

- **Portion Control**: Eating mindfully and controlling portion sizes can prevent overeating and promote a healthier relationship with food.
- **Awareness**: Being aware of the types and quality of food consumed can lead to better dietary choices that support a prophet's physical and spiritual health.

By adopting healthier dietary habits and being mindful of the effects of Western culture's food on their bodies, prophets can better sustain their physical health, mental clarity, and spiritual vitality, enabling them to fulfill their divine calling with greater efficacy and resilience.

Recommended Foods For Prophets

Foods to Eat:

1. *Whole Grains:*
   - o **Examples:** Barley, wheat, oats, millet.
   - o **Benefits:** Provide sustained energy, rich in fiber, and essential nutrients.
2. *Fruits:*
   - o **Examples:** Figs, dates, pomegranates, grapes, apples.
   - o **Benefits:** High in vitamins, minerals, and antioxidants; promote digestion and overall health.
3. *Vegetables:*
   - o **Examples:** Lentils, beans, cucumbers, onions, garlic, leafy greens.
   - o **Benefits:** Packed with vitamins, minerals, and fiber; support immune function and digestion.
4. *Lean Proteins:*
   - o **Examples:** Fish, poultry, eggs.
   - o **Benefits:** Essential for muscle repair and overall body function; fish provides

omega-3 fatty acids beneficial for heart health.

5. *Nuts and Seeds:*
   o **Examples:** Almonds, walnuts, flaxseeds, sesame seeds.
   o **Benefits:** Rich in healthy fats, protein, and fiber; support heart health and provide energy.

6. *Dairy:*
   o **Examples:** Goat's milk, cheese, yogurt.
   o **Benefits:** Source of calcium, protein, and probiotics; support bone health and digestion.

7. *Herbs and Spices:*
   o **Examples:** Mint, coriander, cumin, hyssop.
   o **Benefits:** Enhance flavor and offer various health benefits, including anti-inflammatory and digestive properties.

8. **Natural Sweeteners:**
   o **Examples:** Honey, date syrup.
   o **Benefits:** Provide energy and have antibacterial properties; a better alternative to refined sugars.

Tips for Prophets to Remain Healthy:

1. *Balanced Diet:*
   o Ensure a balanced intake of carbohydrates, proteins, and fats.

- o Include a variety of fruits and vegetables to cover all essential nutrients.

2. *Regular Fasting*:
- o Practice periodic fasting for spiritual and physical cleansing.
- o Follow traditional fasting guidelines to maintain energy and hydration.

3. *Hydration:*
- o Drink plenty of water throughout the day to stay hydrated.
- o Include herbal teas for added benefits and hydration.

4. *Physical Activity:*
- o Engage in regular physical activities such as walking, manual labor, or stretching exercises.
- o Physical activity helps maintain physical strength and mental clarity.

5. *Rest and Meditation:*
- o Ensure adequate rest and sleep to allow the body to recover and rejuvenate.
- o Practice daily meditation and prayer to maintain mental peace and spiritual connection.

6. *Natural Remedies:*
- o Use natural remedies for common ailments, such as herbal teas, poultices, and essential oils.
- o Keep a stock of commonly used herbs and natural medicines.

7. *Mental Health:*

- o Spend time in nature and solitude to reflect and connect with the divine.
- o Engage in community activities to build support networks and maintain emotional well-being.

8. *Regular Cleansing:*
- o Follow regular cleansing rituals, such as bathing and anointing with oils, to maintain hygiene and spiritual purity.
- o A monthly detox would do your body good and provide a safe place for consumption. Herbal detox teas and supplements can provide vitality in your daily routine.
- o Use natural products for personal care.

By adhering to these dietary practices and health tips, prophets can maintain their physical strength, mental clarity, and spiritual attunement, enabling them to fulfill their divine missions effectively.

Food's Effects On The Pineal Gland

For those who have not taken the course, P101-Prophecy 101 with the Ambassadors Institute Of Divinity, you are lacking my teaching on the pineal gland and its function.

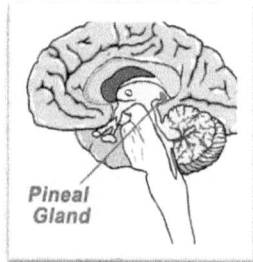

Pineal Gland

The pineal gland, a small endocrine gland in the brain, is responsible for producing melatonin, a hormone that regulates sleep-wake cycles. Certain foods and nutrients can have effects on the pineal gland and its function, primarily through their impact on melatonin production and overall brain health.

Let's go over some of the content in this bonus track of the course prior to my discussion on the pineal gland and its importance. The most important piece of this information is why it is called the 3rd eye.

Why is the pineal gland called the 3rd eye?

*There are several aspects to the pineal gland and how it functions. According to the world's view and understanding of it, it is called the **"Third Eye,"** as it is used for spiritual guidance and direction.*

*The **pineal gland** was commonly dubbed the "**third eye**" for many reasons, including its location deep in the center of the brain and its* *connection to light. Mystic and esoteric spiritual traditions suggest it serves as a metaphysical connection between the physical and spiritual worlds.*

What triggers the pineal gland?

*The **pineal gland** produces several hormones, the most important one is melatonin, which helps to regulate biological rhythms such as wake and sleep cycle. Melatonin secretion **triggered** by darkness and inhibited by light.*

Foods That May Support Pineal Gland Health

Here are some key foods and their effects:

1. **Foods Rich in Tryptophan**:
   o *Examples*: Turkey, chicken, eggs, nuts, seeds, tofu, cheese, and fish.

- ○ *Effect*: Tryptophan is an amino acid that is a precursor to serotonin, which in turn is a precursor to melatonin. Consuming foods high in tryptophan can support melatonin production.

2. **Foods High in Melatonin**:
   - ○ *Examples*: Tart cherries, grapes, strawberries, tomatoes, and nuts (especially walnuts).
   - ○ *Effect:* Directly increases melatonin levels in the body, which can support the natural function of the pineal gland.

3. **Foods Rich in Omega-3 Fatty Acids**:
   - ○ *Examples*: Fatty fish (salmon, mackerel, sardines), flaxseeds, chia seeds, and walnuts.
   - ○ *Effect*: Omega-3 fatty acids support overall brain health and may contribute to the proper functioning of the pineal gland.

4. **Iodine-Rich Foods**:
   - ○ *Examples*: Seaweed, fish, dairy products, and iodized salt.
   - ○ *Effect*: Iodine is essential to produce thyroid hormones, which have a regulatory effect on the pineal gland.

5. **Antioxidant-Rich Foods**:
   - ○ *Examples:* Blueberries, strawberries, dark chocolate, green tea, and leafy greens.

○ *Effect:* Antioxidants help protect the pineal gland from oxidative stress and potential damage from free radicals.

Foods and Substances That May Negatively Affect Pineal Gland Health

1. **Processed Foods and Sugars**:
   ○ *Effect*: High consumption of processed foods and sugars can lead to inflammation and oxidative stress, potentially impacting the pineal gland's function.
2. **Caffeine**:
   ○ *Effect:* Excessive caffeine intake can disrupt sleep patterns and interfere with melatonin production.
3. **Fluoride**:
   ○ *Sources:* Fluoridated water and certain dental products.
   ○ *Effect:* Some studies suggest that high levels of fluoride may accumulate in the pineal gland and potentially affect its function, although this is a subject of ongoing research and debate.
4. **Alcohol**:
   ○ *Effect:* Alcohol consumption can disrupt sleep patterns and interfere with the production and regulation of melatonin.

General Tips for Supporting Pineal Gland Health

- **Maintain a Regular Sleep Schedule**: Consistent sleep patterns support melatonin production.
- **Get Enough Sunlight**: Exposure to natural light during the day helps regulate the sleep-wake cycle.
- **Reduce Exposure to Blue Light**: Minimize exposure to screens and artificial blue light in the evening to support natural melatonin production.
- **Stay Hydrated**: Proper hydration supports overall brain function and health.

By incorporating these dietary practices and lifestyle habits, you can support the health and function of the pineal gland, promoting better sleep and overall well-being.

Handling Pineal Gland Calcification

Pineal gland calcification is the accumulation of calcium deposits in the pineal gland, which can affect its function.

The pineal gland is responsible for producing melatonin, a hormone that regulates sleep-wake cycles. Calcification can potentially disrupt melatonin production and impact overall sleep and circadian rhythm.

Causes of Pineal Gland Calcification:

1. **Aging**: Calcification of the pineal gland is common and tends to increase with age.
2. **Fluoride Exposure**: Some studies suggest that high levels of fluoride exposure might contribute to pineal gland calcification.
3. **Environmental Factors**: Exposure to certain environmental toxins and pollutants may contribute to calcification.
4. **Dietary Factors**: Diets high in processed foods and lacking in essential nutrients might play a role in calcification.

Potential Effects of Pineal Gland Calcification

1. **Disrupted Sleep Patterns**: Reduced melatonin production can lead to sleep disturbances and insomnia.
2. **Circadian Rhythm Disruption**: The body's internal clock might be affected, leading to issues with sleep-wake cycles.
3. **Hormonal Imbalances**: Melatonin plays a role in regulating other hormones, so calcification might lead to broader hormonal imbalances.

Strategies to Reduce Pineal Gland Calcification

Dietary and Lifestyle Changes

1. **Reduce Fluoride Intake**:
   - *Water:* Use a water filter that removes fluoride.
   - *Dental Products*: opt for fluoride-free toothpaste and dental products.
2. **Increase Antioxidant Intake**:
   - *Foods:* Consume foods rich in antioxidants like blueberries, strawberries, dark chocolate, green tea, and leafy greens.
   - *Supplements:* Consider supplements like vitamin C, vitamin E, and glutathione after consulting a healthcare provider.
3. **Magnesium-Rich Foods**:
   - *Sources:* Include foods high in magnesium such as leafy greens, nuts, seeds, whole grains, and dark chocolate.
   - *Effect*: Magnesium helps prevent calcium buildup in tissues.
4. **Iodine-Rich Foods**:
   - *Sources:* Seaweed, fish, dairy products, and iodized salt.
   - *Effect*: Iodine supports thyroid function, which can indirectly affect the pineal gland.

Lifestyle Practices

1. **Sunlight Exposure**:
   - *Effect*: Natural light exposure helps regulate the pineal gland's function and melatonin production.
   - *Recommendation*: Spend time outdoors in natural sunlight during the day.
2. **Reduce Exposure to Blue Light**:
   - *Effect*: Blue light from screens can disrupt melatonin production.
   - *Recommendation*: Minimize screen time, especially before bedtime, and use blue light filters on devices.
3. **Regular Sleep Schedule**:
   - *Effect*: Consistent sleep patterns support the natural production of melatonin.
   - *Recommendation*: Go to bed and wake up at the same time every day.
4. **Detoxification Practices**:
   - *Effect*: Detoxifying the body can help remove environmental toxins that may contribute to calcification.
   - *Recommendation*: Engage in regular physical activity, stay hydrated, and consider detoxifying foods and practices.

Medical Approaches

1. **Chelation Therapy**:
   - ○ **Effect**: Used to remove heavy metals and other toxins from the body.
   - ○ **Recommendation**: Should be done under medical supervision.
2. **Melatonin Supplements**:
   - ○ *Effect*: Can help regulate sleep patterns if natural production is disrupted.
   - ○ *Recommendation*: Consult with a healthcare provider before starting melatonin supplements. This will help determine proper dosages and avoid overdosing.

By adopting these dietary, lifestyle, and medical strategies, it may be possible to reduce the risk or impact of pineal gland calcification, promoting better sleep and overall health.

Decalcify The Pineal Gland:

Cleansing the pineal gland, also known as "decalcifying," the pineal gland, is a concept that involves adopting dietary, lifestyle, and sometimes medical strategies to reduce calcification and improve the function of the pineal gland.

Here are some approaches that people believe can help support the health and function of the pineal gland:

Dietary Strategies

1. **Eliminate Fluoride Intake**:
   - *Water:* Use a water filter that removes fluoride. Do your research on the water you consume, and the chemicals used to purify your water. This may drastically decrease your fluoride intake.
   - *Dental Products*: Use fluoride-free toothpaste and dental products. This includes floss picks if you use them. These are hard to find and can become extremely expensive. It is safe to say if you eliminate fluoride from your toothpaste, a floss pick with fluoride once daily will not hurt as much.
2. **Eat a Nutrient-Rich Diet**:
   - *Magnesium-Rich Foods*: Include leafy greens, nuts, seeds, whole grains, and dark chocolate to help prevent calcium buildup.
   - *Iodine-Rich Foods*: Consume seaweed, fish, dairy products, and iodized salt to support thyroid function.
   - *Antioxidant-Rich Foods*: Incorporate blueberries, strawberries, dark chocolate,

green tea, and leafy greens to protect the pineal gland from oxidative stress.

- ○ ***Chlorella and Spirulina***: These algae are known for their detoxifying properties and may help reduce heavy metal accumulation. Spirulina is also great to feed your thyroid, helping it receive the nutrients it needs to remain healthy.

3. **Reduce Intake of Toxins**:

   - ○ ***Processed   Foods***:   Minimize consumption of processed foods high in additives, preservatives, and artificial ingredients.
   - ○ **Alcohol   and   Caffeine**:   Limit consumption as they can disrupt sleep and affect melatonin production.

Lifestyle Practices

1. **Sunlight Exposure**:

   - ○ Spend time outdoors in natural sunlight during the day to help regulate the pineal gland and support natural melatonin production.

2. **Maintain a Regular Sleep Schedule**:

   - ○ Go to bed and wake up at the same time every day to support consistent melatonin production.

3. **Detoxification Practices**:

- ○ ***Hydration****:* Drink plenty of water to support the body's natural detoxification processes.
- ○ ***Sweating****:* Engage in activities like exercise or sauna sessions to help the body expel toxins through sweat.

4. **Meditation and Relaxation**:
   - ○ Practices like meditation and deep breathing can reduce stress and support overall brain health, including the pineal gland.

Supplements & Natural Remedies

1. **Iodine Supplements**:
   - ○ Consult with a healthcare provider about taking iodine supplements to support thyroid function and overall endocrine health.

2. **Magnesium Supplements**:
   - ○ Consider magnesium supplements to prevent calcium buildup and support overall health.

3. **Melatonin Supplements**:
   - ○ Taking melatonin supplements can help regulate sleep patterns if natural production is disrupted. Consult with a healthcare provider before starting.

4. **Apple Cider Vinegar**:

- o Some believe that apple cider vinegar can help with detoxification. Mix a small amount in water and drink it daily.

5. **Herbs**:
   - o ***Boron***: Found in foods like nuts, grapes, and avocados, and sometimes taken as a supplement.
   - o ***Chaga Mushroom***: Believed to have detoxifying properties.
   - o ***Neem Extract***: Often used for its potential to cleanse the body.

Medical Approaches

1. **Chelation Therapy**:
   - o A medical treatment that involves the administration of chelating agents to remove heavy metals from the body. This should only be done under the supervision of a healthcare provider.

While scientific evidence supporting the effectiveness of these methods specifically for "decalcifying" the pineal gland is limited, these practices can contribute to overall health and well-being.

It's important to consult with a healthcare provider before starting any new supplement or significant dietary or lifestyle change. By adopting a holistic approach that includes a healthy diet, proper hydration, regular sleep, and stress reduction, you can support the health of your pineal gland and overall brain function.

Initially, when I learned the 'power' of the pineal gland, I searched for easy ways to perform a cleansing. I have included the recipe for the smoothie I drank on a very regular basis to assist with decalcification.

There are no measurements, you will have to measure according to your eye and how much you plan to drink in one sitting. 😊

PINEAL POWER SMOOTHIE:

- Watercress
- Banana
- Avocado
- Pineapple
- Coconut Water

Determine the portions according to how much you plan to drink. To maintain freshness, only make as much as you can consume in one sitting. This should be performed at least 2-3 times per week to maintain sharpness.

CHAPTER 4:

The Prophet's Garments

In the context of fabrics and their interaction with the body's energy field, the idea of fabrics yielding a "high frequency" refers to the belief in holistic and alternative health practices that certain materials can positively influence or harmonize the body's energy.

Here are some fabrics that are often mentioned in this context:

1. **Silk**: Known for its luxurious feel, silk is often believed to have a high vibrational frequency. It is said to have calming and harmonizing effects on the body and mind.
2. **Linen**: Linen is a natural fiber that is highly regarded in holistic health circles. It is believed

to have healing properties and a high frequency, promoting a sense of well-being and vitality.

3. **Wool**: Wool, especially when untreated and natural, is considered to have good vibrational properties. It is thought to provide warmth and grounding energy.

4. **Cotton**: While not always as highly praised as linen or silk, cotton is a natural fiber that is breathable and comfortable. Organic cotton is often recommended for its purity and lack of chemical treatments.

5. **Hemp**: Hemp fabric is gaining popularity for its durability and environmental benefits. It is also considered to have a positive energy frequency, promoting balance and wellness.

6. **Bamboo**: Bamboo fabric is praised for its softness, sustainability, and natural antibacterial properties. It is believed to have a soothing and harmonizing effect on the body.

These beliefs are rooted in the idea that natural fibers, untreated with chemicals, have a more beneficial effect on the body's energy field compared to synthetic materials. It is important to note that while these ideas are popular in certain holistic and alternative health communities, they are not widely accepted or supported by mainstream science.

However, some say that linen and wool should not be worn together because their frequencies run in opposite directions and cancel each other out.

In contrast, synthetic fabrics like polyester, nylon, and acrylic may have lower frequencies and a negative effect on the body.

MHz (MEGA HERTZ) = FREQUENCY

In 2003 a Jewish doctor, Heidi Yellen, did a study on the frequencies of fabrics, in which she showed that a healthy human body has a signature frequency of 100, and wearing a material that measures less than 100 units of energy would compromise our wellbeing. Each fabric gives a frequency that can be measured in MHz (megaHertZ).

MHz Measurements:

- Organic cotton has a tested value of 110 MHz.
- Polyester is around 10 MHz.
- A diseased person generally measures 15 MHz.
- Wool and Linen both have a signature of 5000 MHz.

The amazing naturally created feature of the fabrics will also give energy to your body as you wear it. It is important however to not wear linen and wool together as the frequencies in both of the linen and wool fibers run in opposite current directions. If you wear them together, the two frequencies will cancel each other out and bring you to a 0.

Healing Properties
Of Each Fabric:

Silk has many healing properties, including:

- **Wound healing**: Silk is often used in wound care because it can promote cell attachment, migration, and collagen deposition. It can also help soothe irritated skin and enhance healing by facilitating moisture.
- **Antibacterial and antifungal**: Silk contains sericin, a protein that has antibacterial and antifungal properties. This can help repel dust mites and mold.
- **Hypoallergenic**: Silk is naturally hypoallergenic, making it ideal for people with sensitive skin or breathing conditions.
- **Temperature regulation**: Silk can help regulate body temperature and reduce excessive sweating.
- **Hair health**: Sleeping on a silk pillowcase can help prevent hair tangling and breakage.

Linen has many healing properties, including:

- **Breathable**: Linen's hollow fibers allow for better airflow than other fabrics.
- **Hypoallergenic**: Linen is good for people with sensitive skin. Flax, the material linen is made from, contains silica, which prevents bacteria

that causes fermentation from growing. Linen also dries faster than cotton, which prevents bacteria from building up. In the past, hospitals used linen for bandages and sheets to help wounds heal faster and reduce the risk of infection.

- **Antistatic**: Linen's antistatic properties prevent it from attracting dust.

Linen also has other health benefits, including odor-resistant, stimulates healthy blood flow, reduces the risk of fungal diseases, and neutralizes the smell of sweat or damp towels.

Linen is also considered eco-friendly because it's recyclable and biodegradable. It's also easy to maintain and doesn't require special washing or drying instructions.

Wool has many healing properties, including:

- **Temperature regulation**: Wool can help you stay comfortable in any weather.
- **Insulation**: Wool can absorb up to 35% of its weight in moisture, keeping you warm even when it's damp. Wool shoes can also keep your feet warm in winter and cool in summer.

- **Cooling**: Wool can help cool you down when your body temperature rises and keep you warm when it drops.
- **Pain relief**: Wool can increase circulation, which can help with pain. Wool products can also conform to your body and relieve pressure points, which can be comforting for people with chronic pain, arthritis, or fibromyalgia.
- **Antibacterial**: Wool contains lanolin, a waxy coating that contains fatty acids with antibacterial properties. These fatty acids can inhibit the growth of bacteria, which can help wool products stay cleaner and smell better for longer.
- **Moisture-wicking**: Wool can draw moisture away from your skin and to the surface of the fabric, where it can evaporate. This can help prevent blisters and keep your feet dry and comfortable.
- **UV protection**: Wool can absorb harmful UV rays, with an Ultraviolet Protection Factor (UPF) typically between 20 and 50.
- **Blood flow:** Sheepskin can stimulate blood flow, which can help people who are cold at night and with other illnesses. For example, praying with an organic sheepskin blanket or sitting on this type of rug can be beneficial.
- **Skin conditions**: Wool helps with skin conditions. A study of babies and young children in Melbourne showed Merino wool

base layers had significant advantages in improving the symptoms of eczema in comparison to cotton. They documented significantly reduced skin irritations, and an improvement in mental and physical wellbeing.

Cotton has many healing properties, including:

- **Wound healing**: Cotton-based alginate dressings can help wounds heal by forming a soft gel when they meet wound fluid, which keeps the wound moist. The dressings are also absorbent and can conform to the shape and size of the wound, while still allowing for movement around joints.
- **Hypoallergenic**: Cotton is natural and hypoallergenic, making it a good choice for people with sensitive skin.
- **Reduces risk of infection**: Cotton is breathable and absorbs moisture, which can help keep you dry and lower your risk of yeast infections.
- **Keeps you cool**: Cotton's breathability can help keep you cool on hot days.
- **Helps you sleep**: Unlike synthetic fibers like polyester, cotton won't trap heat underneath your covers, which can help you sleep.

Hemp fabric has many healing properties, including:

Pure hemp fiber has a texture like linen. It can also be used with other natural fibers to create clothing with the strength of hemp but the softness of cotton or bamboo.

Hemp fabric is resilient, pleasant, and environmentally friendly because it is made completely of natural fibers. The fabric is also antimicrobial, hypoallergenic, and anti-static. So, let's plunge into the full list of hemp clothes benefits.

- **Strong & durable**: The clothing's actual worth is determined by its durability and strength. Hemp clothing offers three to four times the strength of cotton clothes. It is one of hemp fabrics' distinguishing features, and it sets it apart from conventional garments.
- **Breathable & insulating**: Some materials are designed to keep you warm in the winter and cool in the summer, but only a few can do both. Hemp clothing, like bamboo, performs the same effect. The cellulose strands in hemp clothes have a unique structure that allows them to breathe. Hemp clothing can preserve your true body temperature, which is a significant advantage. This applies to hemp bed sheets, blankets, and pillows, as well as hemp clothes. Hemp and bamboo bed sheets are far superior to cotton ones.

- **Antimicrobial**: We have all experienced that weird odor that comes from garments that have not been washed in a while or have sat in the washer for too long. This is not the case with hemp clothing because of its natural antibacterial characteristics. This super-plant has a lot of superpowers! Because hemp clothing is naturally antibacterial, it can keep its scent for longer while also resisting mold and mildew. When opposed to conventional textiles like cotton, this preserves your hemp clothing, as well as the surrounding clothes, from becoming smelly and staying fresh for a long time.

- **Biodegradable**: There are instances when our garments become permanently damaged or simply worn out beyond repair. Unfortunately, this means you will not be able to give it to a family member, friend, or charity. Hemp clothing is 100% organically biodegradable, so it is not the end of the world if you throw it away. Obviously, no one likes to throw their clothes away, but it does happen, even to the best of clothes. It is preferable to have clothes that are naturally biodegradable. Clothes that are not naturally biodegradable may spend a long period in a landfill.

- **Highly Renewable**: Hemp is a renewable resource that grows quickly. Hemp can be harvested up to three times each year and matures in as little as 120 days. In comparison to cotton, hemp may produce 200-250% more fiber on the same amount of land. What is more, hemp will thrive on the ground that is not suitable for other plants. This also implies that hemp does not have to use up valuable farmland for food, which is always a challenge. Cotton, forests, and other natural resources that we use for clothing and other commodities grow at a slower rate than hemp. Not only is this beneficial to productivity, but it is also necessary for environmental health to quickly regenerate land and soil after each harvest. Because hemp helps to repair soil, it can be used to grow plants that require healthier soil and a longer time to thrive.

- **Versatile**: Hemp fabric may be used for nearly everything, from underwear to drapes to laptop bags to furniture, and its qualities make it an excellent mixing fabric. As a result, hemp may be used with practically any other fabric to produce a wide range of garments. Hemp fibers can be woven alone or in combination with other materials to create everything from canvas to gauze. The incredible strength of hemp fibers is preserved in these hemp-hybrid textiles, which are softer and prettier. Hemp silk is the most luxurious of them all.

- **<u>Odor Resistant</u>**: Hemp clothing, unlike cotton, does not retain body odor due to its natural moisture-wicking properties. Hemp clothing is an excellent choice if you want to smell good all day. Hemp cloth is resistant to mildew and mold because of its antibacterial characteristics, and it absorbs moisture. Many people wonder if hemp garments maintain the plant's odor. They do not.

Bamboo fabric has many healing properties that can be beneficial for the skin and overall well-being.

Bamboo fabric has many healing properties, including:

- ***<u>Antibacterial</u>:*** Bamboo fibers can kill up to 70% of bacteria, repelling mold, mildew, and other types of bacteria. This can help prevent the spread of disease and keep you feeling and smelling fresh, even after many hours of wear. Bamboo's antibacterial properties also make it good for sensitive skin, as it can help prevent irritation and allergies.
- ***<u>Hypoallergenic</u>:*** Bamboo is an all-natural, hypoallergenic fabric that's soothing against scarred, wounded, or damaged skin.
- ***<u>UV protective</u>:*** Bamboo can filter up to 97.5% of the sun's UV rays, making it a great choice for keeping your skin safe from sun damage during the summer months.

- ***Moisture-wicking****:* Bamboo is naturally moisture-wicking, making it great for activewear, underwear, sleepwear, and more.
- ***Breathable****:* Bamboo bed sheets are highly breathable, allowing air to circulate through the fibers, which is ideal for warmer months.

The Priest's Garments In The Old Testament

After exploring modern-day fabrics and their benefits, let's delve into the fabrics used by the priests of old when constructing their garments. Understanding the parallel usage of these materials will illuminate why the Most High specifically instructed their use.

In the Old Testament, particularly in the book of Exodus, the garments worn by the priests were described in great detail. These garments were made from specific fabrics and materials as prescribed by God.

Here are the key fabrics and materials used for the priests' garments:

Linen: The primary fabric used for the priests' garments was linen. Linen is a natural fiber made from the flax plant. It is mentioned specifically in several parts of Exodus as the fabric for the tunics, undergarments, and the turban of the priests (**Exodus 28:39-42**).

<u>**Gold, Blue, Purple, and Scarlet Yarns**</u>: These were used in conjunction with fine linen for making the ephod, the breast piece, and other parts of the high priest's garments (**Exodus 28:6, 8, 15**). The yarns were intricately woven into the linen fabric to create beautiful and meaningful designs.

<u>**Fine Twined Linen**</u>: This term refers to linen that was particularly finely spun and of high quality. It was used for various parts of the high priest's attire, including the ephod and the breast piece (**Exodus 28:15**).

<u>**Embroidery and Weaving**</u>: Skilled craftsmanship was used to create the intricate designs on the garments. The linen fabrics were often embroidered with threads of gold, blue, purple, and scarlet (**Exodus 28:39**).

The combination of these fabrics and materials made the priests' garments not only beautiful but also rich in symbolic meaning, representing purity, holiness, and the glory of God. The specific instructions for the design and materials of these garments can be found in Exodus 28 and 39.

In addition to the fabrics used to make the priest's garments, the ephod was also of intricate design. It is important to note the stones used in the ephod as each stone has healing properties. The design and details was given by the Most High, which means he understood the meaning of each stone.

While we do not endorse using stones as a substitute for the Holy Spirit, it is important to recognize their natural healing properties, which can be used to support physical healing and prophetic well-being. Stones should not be worn to ward off spirits or to maintain your "energy"—those are roles of the Holy Spirit. However, stones can be used as a tool to aid the body in healing from ailments. When combined with herbs, stones can contribute to promoting health and vitality.

The Priest's Ephod (Old Testament)

There were 12 stones across the breastplate of the priest. Let's look at each stone and their spiritual meaning.

The priest's ephod in the Old Testament, specifically the breastplate worn by the High Priest, contained twelve stones. Each stone represented one of the twelve tribes of Israel. Here is a list of the stones and their spiritual connotations:

1. **Ruby (Reuben)**

- o **Spiritual Connotation:** Symbolizes blood, sacrifice, and redemption. Ruby is associated with courage, passion, and love.
- o **Healing Properties:**
    1. Boosts energy.
    2. Strengthens the heart and improves circulation.
    3. Enhances concentration and motivation

2. **Topaz (Simeon)**
   - o **Spiritual Connotation:** Represents divine favor, healing, and wisdom. Topaz is often associated with clarity of thought and purpose.
   - o **Healing Properties:**

       1. Balances emotions and promotes relaxation.
       2. Enhances the immune system and metabolism.
       3. Supports healthy digestion.

3. **Emerald (Levi)**
   - o **Spiritual Connotation:** Signifies eternal life, immortality, and faithfulness. Emerald is linked to renewal, growth, and hope.
   - o **Healing Properties:**
       1. Supports heart health and aids in recovery from illnesses.

    2. Enhances vision and eye health.

4. **Turquoise (Judah)**
   - **Spiritual Connotation:** Represents protection, guidance, and leadership. Turquoise is seen as a symbol of power and status.
   - **Healing Properties:**
     1. Supports respiratory health and alleviates throat issues.
     2. Promotes communication and self-expression.

5. **Sapphire (Issachar)**
   - **Spiritual Connotation:** Symbolizes divine favor, loyalty, and wisdom. Sapphire is associated with purity, holiness, and divine insight.
   - **Healing Properties:**
     1. Supports overall eye health and vision.
     2. Calms the mind and relieves stress.

6. **Diamond (Zebulun)**

   - **Spiritual Connotation:** Represents strength, clarity, and invincibility. Diamonds are a symbol of purity, righteousness, and endurance.
   - **Healing Properties:**
     1. Supports detoxification and purification.

2. Strengthens the brain and nerves.

7. **Jacinth (Dan)**
   o **Spiritual Connotation:** Signifies discernment, wisdom, and judgment. Jacinth is associated with protection and spiritual insight.
   o **Healing Properties:**
     1. Supports the body's metabolic functions.
     2. Aids in emotional healing and stability.

8. **Agate (Naphtali)**
   o **Spiritual Connotation:** Represents stability, grounding, and inner strength. Agate is linked to balance, harmony, and protection.
   o **Healing Properties:**
     1. Improves concentration and analytical abilities.
     2. Heals skin disorders and strengthens the immune system.

9. **Amethyst (Gad)**
   o **Spiritual Connotation:** Symbolizes peace, protection, and divine connection. Amethyst is often associated with spiritual awareness and sobriety.
   o **Healing Properties:**

1. Supports sleep and alleviates insomnia.
2. Aids in overcoming addictions and promotes sobriety

10. Beryl (Asher)

o **Spiritual Connotation:** Represents divine favor, wealth, and abundance. Beryl is seen as a symbol of happiness and prosperity.
o **Healing Properties:**
   1. Supports liver and kidney function.
   2. Promotes creativity and eliminates distractions.

11. Onyx (Joseph/Ephraim and Manasseh)

o **Spiritual Connotation:** Signifies strength, stability, and endurance. Onyx is linked to protection, willpower, and self-control.
o **Healing Properties:**

   1. Promotes stamina, self-control, and emotional balance.
   2. Aids in physical recovery and healing from past trauma.

12. Jasper (Benjamin)

- o **Spiritual Connotation:** Symbolizes endurance, perseverance, and healing. Jasper is associated with grounding, protection, and stability.
- o **Health Properties:**

  1. Supports physical strength and endurance.
  2. Aids in detoxification and cleansing of the body.

These stones, set in the High Priest's breastplate, not only represented the twelve tribes of Israel but also carried deep spiritual meanings that underscored the covenant relationship between God and His people.

The Garments Of Yeshua

The Bible does not provide detailed descriptions of the specific fabrics used in Jesus' garments. However, based on historical and cultural context, we can infer the likely materials:

1. **Linen**: Linen was a common fabric in ancient Israel, used for both everyday clothing and religious garments. It is reasonable to assume that some of Jesus' clothing could have been made from linen.
2. **Wool**: Wool was another common material for clothing in ancient times. It was durable

and provided warmth, making it a practical choice for everyday wear.

3. **Cotton**: While less common than linen and wool, cotton was known in the region and might have been used for some garments.

Specific Garments Mentioned:

- **Seamless Tunic**: One of the few specific references to Jesus' clothing is the seamless tunic He wore at the time of His crucifixion. In John 19:23-24, it is described as woven in one piece from top to bottom. This suggests a garment of high quality, possibly made from fine linen or wool.

Cultural and Historical Context:

- **Simple and Modest Clothing**: Jesus is often depicted as wearing simple, modest clothing typical of His time and social standing. This would include a tunic (chiton) worn under a cloak (himation), both likely made from linen or wool.
- **Traditional Jewish Attire**: As a Jewish man, Jesus would have worn garments that complied with Jewish customs, including tassels (tzitzit) on the corners of His cloak as commanded in the Torah (**Numbers 15:38-39; Deuteronomy 22:12**).

Overall, while the Bible does not specify the exact fabrics of Jesus' garments, historical context suggests they were made from common materials like linen and wool, reflecting the clothing customs of His time and culture.

I am sure you may be wondering, what does 'clothing' have to do with a prophet's diet. Well, as in the title of this book, we are meant to create 'lifestyles' as prophets. If you cannot see the significance of clothing with your diet, then you need to return to this chapter and read it a few more times.

$\mathcal{H}$ebrew $\mathcal{T}$reasure

"You shall keep my statutes: do not breed any of your domestic animals with others of a different species; do not sow a field of yours with two different kinds of seed; and do not put on a garment woven with two different kinds of thread."

— $\mathcal{L}$eviticus 19:19

CHAPTER 5:

The Prophet's Body Care & Well Being

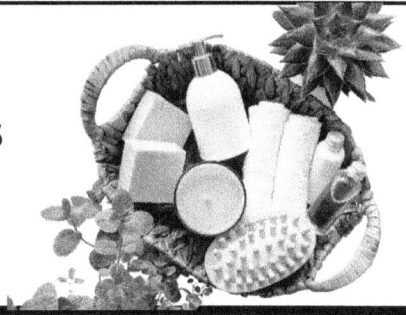

Caring for the body is essential for maintaining the physical, mental, and spiritual well-being of anyone, including a prophet. Here are some holistic practices and guidelines to ensure comprehensive body care:

Physical Health

Nutrition:

- **Balanced Diet**: Consume a diet rich in fruits, vegetables, whole grains, lean proteins, and healthy fats.
- *Hydration*: Drink plenty of water to stay hydrated and support bodily functions.

- ***Avoid Harmful Substances***: Limit or avoid caffeine, alcohol, and processed foods.

Exercise:

- ***Regular Physical Activity***: Engage in regular exercise such as walking, jogging, or swimming, to maintain physical fitness and reduce stress.
- ***Stretching***: Incorporate stretching exercises to maintain flexibility and prevent injuries.

Sleep:

- ***Consistent Sleep Schedule***: Aim for 7-9 hours of sleep per night and maintain a regular sleep schedule.
- ***Sleep Environment***: Create a restful environment free of distractions and conducive to quality sleep.

Hygiene:

- ***Personal Hygiene***: Maintain good personal hygiene by bathing regularly, brushing and flossing teeth, and keeping nails trimmed.
- ***Clean Environment***: Keep living and working spaces clean and organized.

Mental Health

Stress Management:

- *Mindfulness and Meditation*: Practice mindfulness, meditation, or prayer regularly to reduce stress and maintain mental clarity.
- *Relaxation Techniques*: Engage in activities that promote relaxation, such as deep breathing exercises, listening to calming music, or spending time in nature.

Mental Stimulation:

- *Continuous Learning*: Keep the mind active through reading, studying, and learning new skills or knowledge.
- *Creative Activities*: Engage in creative activities like writing, painting, or playing a musical instrument.

Spiritual Health

Prayer and Meditation:

- *Regular Prayer*: Maintain a consistent prayer routine to stay connected with God and seek guidance.

- **Meditative Practices**: Incorporate meditation to reflect on spiritual teachings and cultivate inner peace.

Community and Service:

- **Fellowship**: Participate in community and church activities to build supportive relationships and spiritual growth.
- **Service**: Engage in acts of service and charity to live out spiritual values and help others.

Emotional Health

Emotional Expression:

- *Healthy Outlets*: Find healthy outlets for emotions such as journaling, talking to a trusted friend or mentor, or engaging in creative activities.
- *Counseling*: Seek counseling or therapy if needed to process emotions and manage mental health challenges.

Relationships:

- *Healthy Relationships*: Foster healthy, supportive relationships with family, friends, and community members.

- *Boundaries*: Establish and maintain healthy boundaries to protect emotional and mental well-being.

Specific Considerations For Prophets

Discernment:

- *Time for Reflection*: Set aside time for reflection and discernment to seek clarity and guidance on prophetic insights and messages.
- *Spiritual Guidance*: Seek mentorship or guidance from experienced spiritual leaders.

Balance:

- *Work-Life Balance*: Maintain a balance between prophetic duties and personal life to prevent burnout and ensure overall well-being.
- *Sabbath Rest*: Observe periods of rest and rejuvenation, such as taking a weekly Sabbath.

By incorporating these practices, a prophet can maintain a healthy body, mind, and spirit, allowing them to fulfill their calling effectively and sustainably.

The issue of a lifestyle change is more than going Vegan or changing what you eat. It is inclusive of cleansing out your personal care products, watching what you use and apply to your body. Remembering *I Corinthians 3:16*, let's monitor the upkeep of our temples.

Here are some other items that you need to explore replacing:

- Deodorants
- Toothpaste
- Mouthwash
- Water (certain bottled waters cleansed with fluoride)
- Processed foods (made with water that contains fluoride)
- Body lotions & creams
- Items that contain fluoride
- Soaps, body washes & shower gels

To cleanse the body, decalcify your pineal gland and maintain a higher frequency, which heightens your spiritual awareness, you absolutely need to take into close consideration what you absorb into your body. What you put on your body and your environment plays a major role in your spirituality.

A lifestyle change is not *just* what you eat, but

everything that goes along with being in total and complete health and healing.

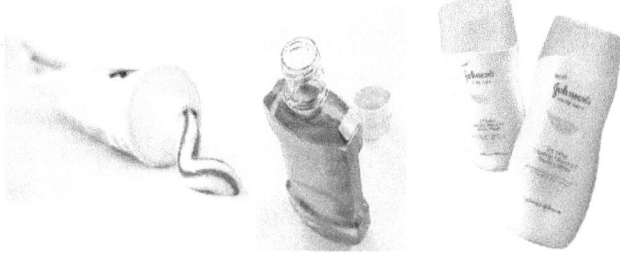

(**Source:** Bonus Track-The 3rd Eye Study-Prophecy 101, By: Apostle Audrea V. Abraham)

*H*ebrew *T*reasure

"Having therefore

these promises, dearly

beloved, let us cleanse

ourselves from all filthiness

of the flesh and spirit,

perfecting holiness in the

fear of God."

— 2 *C*orinthians 7:1

CHAPTER 6:

The Prophet's Mental Health

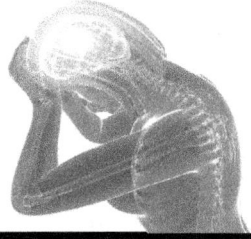

One of the challenges I've observed with prophets is their inability to ward off mental attacks. It appears that a common reality for prophets is that they face numerous mental struggles.

In the annals of ancient history, prophets are often depicted as towering figures of spiritual strength and wisdom, their lives interwoven with divine purpose and celestial guidance. Yet, behind the veil of their prophetic missions, they were also human beings susceptible to the frailties and ailments that afflict all of humanity.

This chapter delves into the intricate tapestry of a prophet's health, exploring the physical and mental challenges they faced while carrying the weight of their divine calling.

The health of a prophet was not merely a personal matter but a significant aspect of their ability to fulfill their mission. Their well-being often reflected the broader societal and environmental conditions of their time, from the scourges of disease to the effects of famine and warfare. By examining the health of prophets, we gain a deeper understanding of the resilience and perseverance required to navigate their extraordinary paths.

Through this exploration, we aim to humanize the prophets, while giving practical insight and instructions to maintain mental health clarity.

Maintaining mental health is crucial for prophets, given their unique role in providing spiritual guidance and support to others. Let's explore strategies and considerations to ensure the mental well-being of prophets.

Spiritual Practices

Regular Prayer and Meditation

- *Daily Prayer*: Engage in regular prayer to seek strength, guidance, and comfort from God.

- *Meditation*: Practice meditation to quiet the mind, reflect on spiritual insights, and cultivate inner peace.

Scriptural Study

- *Bible Study:* Dedicate time to studying the Bible and other sacred texts for spiritual nourishment and guidance.
- *Reflection:* Reflect on scriptural teachings and how they apply to personal life and prophetic mission.

Emotional & Psychological Care

Counseling and Mentorship

- **Seek Counseling**: Engage in regular sessions with a counselor or therapist to process emotions and address mental health concerns. Let's normalize seeking a therapist when needed and prayer when the therapist is needed less.
- *Mentorship:* Establish a relationship with a trusted mentor or spiritual advisor for guidance and support.

Emotional Expression

- *Journaling:* Write in a journal to express thoughts and emotions and gain clarity on personal experiences. I am a huge advocate of journaling as the mind can race at a mile a minute sometimes. You will learn when you write it down, you will have less of a need to 'talk' with someone. This does not outweigh the need for human insight into your situation, but you would be surprised at how God will speak to your written words.
- *Creative Outlets:* Participate in creative activities such as writing, painting, or music to process and express emotions.

Stress Management

Mindfulness and Relaxation Techniques

- *Mindfulness Practices*: Incorporate mindfulness techniques, such as deep breathing exercises to stay present and manage stress.
- *Relaxation Techniques:* Engage in relaxation practices such as spending time in nature to reduce stress and promote mental well-being.

Balanced Lifestyle

- *Work-Life Balance*: Ensure a healthy balance between prophetic duties and personal life to prevent burnout.
- *Sabbath Rest:* Observe regular periods of rest, such as taking a weekly Sabbath, to rejuvenate and maintain overall well-being. While this was mentioned previously, I can not speak more to the need to incorporate sabbath rest. It is an excellent time of reflection and fellowship with the Most High.

Community and Relationships

Supportive Relationships

- *Healthy Relationships*: Foster supportive and healthy relationships with family, friends, and community members.
- *Communication*: Maintain open and honest communication with loved ones to build strong, supportive networks.

Community Involvement

- *Fellowship:* Participate in community and church activities to build connections and receive communal support.
- *Service:* Engage in acts of service and charity to fulfill spiritual duties and connect with others meaningfully.

101

Self-Care Practices

Physical Health

- *Exercise*: Engage in regular physical activity to support overall health and reduce stress.
- *Nutrition*: Maintain a balanced diet rich in essential nutrients to support mental and physical health.
- *Sleep*: Ensure adequate and quality sleep to support cognitive function and emotional well-being.

Hobbies and Interests

- *Personal Interests*: Pursue hobbies and activities that bring joy and relaxation.
- *Leisure Time*: Schedule regular leisure time to unwind and recharge.

Professional Development

Continuous Learning

- *Education*: Pursue ongoing education and training in areas relevant to prophetic work and personal interests.
- *Skill Development*: Develop skills that support mental health, such as

communication, conflict resolution, and stress management.

Coping Strategies

Crisis Management

- *Preparedness:* Develop a plan for managing crises and stressful situations, including identifying support resources and coping strategies.
- *Resilience Building*: Cultivate resilience through practices such as positive thinking, problem-solving, and seeking support when needed.

Self-Compassion

- *Kindness to Self*: Practice self-compassion by treating oneself with kindness and understanding, especially during challenging times.
- *Acceptance:* Accept imperfections and limitations as part of human experience and seek growth and improvement without self-judgment.

By incorporating these strategies, prophets can maintain their mental health, ensuring they are equipped to fulfill their spiritual calling while also caring for their personal well-being.

CHAPTER 7:

The Prophet's Archetype

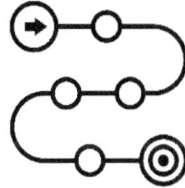

Inside this chapter, we will look at the archetype, or avatar of the prophet. In totality, it will serve as the model for the prophet's diet and what this lifestyle looks like according to Yeshua's design.

This outline is bare now, but we will complete what it should look like in your life by the end of this chapter. This will be your conclusion on the matter!

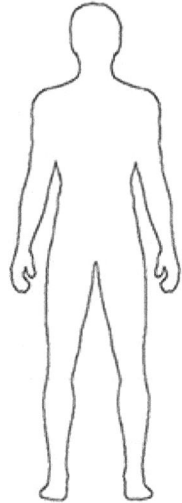

A QUICK REVIEW...

The prophets of ancient Israel were not only the mouthpieces of the divine but also paragons of holistic living. Their lives, marked by simplicity and spiritual dedication, offer profound insights into the interplay between diet, health, and spiritual well-being. We will delve into the archetype of the prophet, examining the comprehensive lifestyle practices that underpinned their ability to fulfill their sacred duties.

Inside this chapter, we will look at the archetype, or what is known as the avatar of the prophet. In totality, it will serve as the model for the prophet's diet and what this lifestyle looks like according to Yeshua's design.

Understanding the dietary practices in ancient Israel is crucial to grasping how prophets maintained their physical and spiritual health. Their diets were influenced by religious laws and cultural traditions, emphasizing foods that were clean, simple, and nourishing. By exploring the specific diets of notable prophets, we uncovered how these figures used food not just for sustenance but as a means to enhance their spiritual connection and physical resilience.

The effects of food on the body were well-understood by these ancient seers, who selected their meals with a keen awareness of how different foods impacted their health and vitality. The right diet was seen as essential for maintaining a body that could endure the physical demands of prophetic missions and the mental clarity required for divine communication.

The garments worn by prophets were more than just clothing; they were symbols of their divine mission and personal commitment to a life of purity and service. Each element of their attire, from the humble robe to the intricate ephod, carried deep spiritual significance and practical function.

Body care and well-being practices among prophets extended beyond diet and clothing. Rituals of cleansing and anointing, the use of natural remedies, and the incorporation of physical exercise were all integral to their daily routines. These practices ensured that their bodies remained strong, and their spirits unburdened, ready to receive and deliver divine messages.

Finally, the mental lifestyle of a prophet was characterized by disciplines that fostered inner peace and spiritual attunement. Meditation, prayer, and periods of solitude were essential for maintaining the mental clarity and emotional stability needed to navigate their prophetic roles.

We will weave together the diverse threads of the prophet's archetype to create a rich tapestry of the prophet's lifestyle. By understanding the holistic approach to health and well-being embraced by these ancient figures, we gain deeper insight into their extraordinary lives and the enduring legacy of their wisdom.

The Archetype In Motion

1. Dietary Practices in Ancient Israel: Adhering to the traditional dietary practices of ancient Israel, which are deeply rooted in religious and cultural customs promote spiritual discipline. This diet primarily consists of grains, fruits, vegetables, legumes, and fish, with occasional consumption of meat, mainly during religious feasts. Following the laws of kashrut, ensures all food is ritually pure. Avoiding forbidden foods like pork and shellfish along with practicing regular fasting is a lifestyle according to Yeshua's design.

2. Specific Prophets & Their Diets: Your diet can be influenced by the dietary habits of notable prophets such as Elijah, who was sustained by simple meals like bread and water during his wilderness sojourns, and Daniel, who famously adhered to a diet of vegetables and water to maintain purity. Like these prophets, you can experience the simplicity of natural foods, believing that such a diet helps maintain physical purity and spiritual clarity.

3. Food's Effects on the Body: After reading this book, you should be aware of how food affects your body and overall well-being. Choosing foods that are believed to promote health and vitality, such as figs for their energy-boosting properties and honey for its healing benefits will promote your vitality. Avoid overindulgence, recognizing that moderation is key to maintaining a body that can endure the rigors of your prophetic mission.

4. The Prophet's Garments: Your attire should reflect your role and commitment as a prophet to humility and service. Wearing simple, yet distinctive robes made from coarse, undyed wool symbolizes purity and asceticism. Your garments should be functional, allowing ease of movement, and durable enough to withstand your travels and the various conditions you may face.

5. The Prophet's Body Care & Well-Being: You should maintain a disciplined routine for body care and well-being. Practice regular cleansing rituals, often using natural ingredients like olive oil and herbs for anointing and purification. The healing power of natural remedies and preparing herbal infusions will help treat ailments. Physical exercise through walking and manual labor should be an integral part of your daily life, ensuring your body remains strong and resilient.

6. The Prophet's Mental Lifestyle: Mental clarity and emotional stability are paramount to your prophetic duties. Engaging in daily meditation and prayer, while seeking communion with the Most High will ground you in your spiritual mission.

Practicing mindfulness, remaining present in each moment and attuned to the subtle messages from the Most High will keep you on course to your prophetic assignment. Retreating to solitary places to reflect and recharge, understanding that a tranquil mind is essential for receiving and interpreting prophetic visions.

Embodying the archetype of a prophet means that through disciplined dietary practices, simple yet significant attire, meticulous body care, and a mentally enriching lifestyle will give you success in your endeavors. This holistic approach to health and well-being ensures that you remain a steadfast vessel for divine communication, carrying out your prophetic duties with clarity, strength, and unwavering faith.

Review the prophet archetype on the next page to see everything we have reviewed come together.

THE PROPHET'S DIET

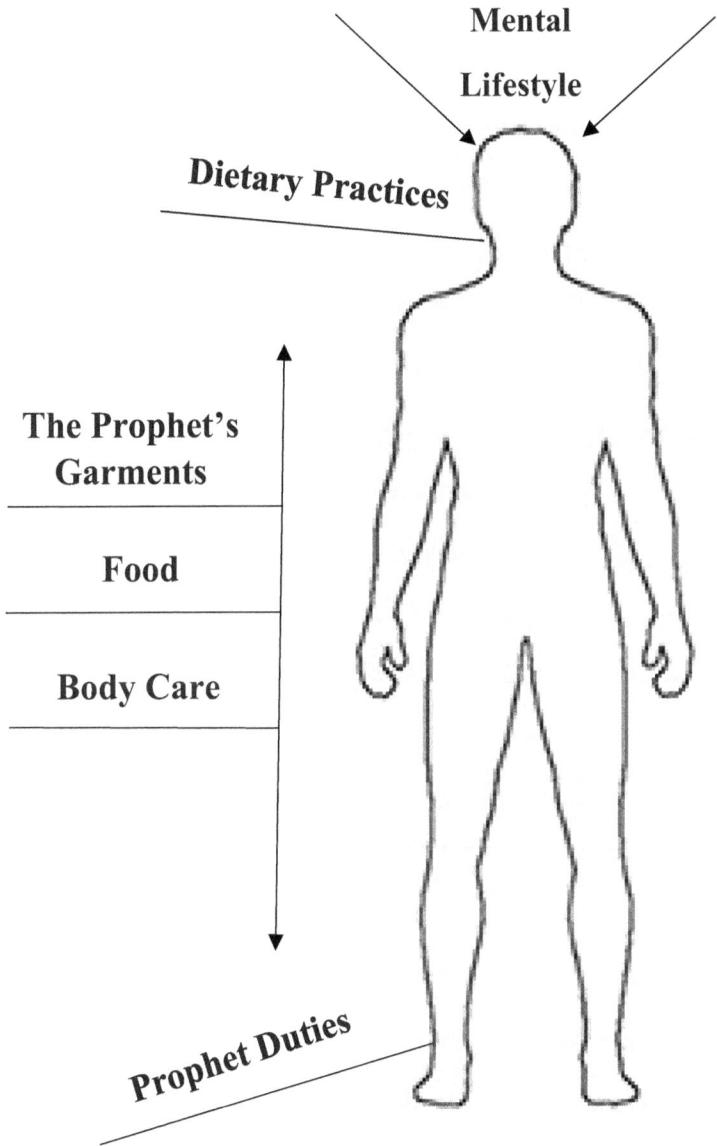

Mental

Lifestyle

Dietary Practices

The Prophet's
Garments

Food

Body Care

Prophet Duties

A. Summary of Key Points:

- **Dietary Practices in Ancient Israel**: Explored the kosher laws, common foods, and cultural significance of food in biblical times.
- **Specific Prophets and Their Diets**: Examined the diets of Elijah, Daniel, Ezekiel, and John the Baptist, Jesus and other New Testament prophets, highlighting their dependence on God, symbolic acts, and lessons on simplicity and faith.
- **Symbolism and Lessons**: Emphasized the prophets' reliance on God, acts of obedience, lessons on self-denial, and dietary practices as expressions of faith and commitment.
- **Comparison with New Testament Teachings**: Discussed Jesus' teachings on clean and unclean foods, His miracles involving food, and Paul's teachings on freedom in Christ and respecting others' dietary choices.

B. Reflection on the Relevance of Prophets' Diets for Modern Readers:

- **Faith and Trust**: Modern readers can draw inspiration from the prophets' trust in God's provision, reminding them to rely on God in times of need.

- **Obedience and Commitment**: The prophets' adherence to specific diets as acts of obedience encourages believers to remain committed to their faith and values, even when faced with challenges.
- **Simplicity and Self-Denial**: The emphasis on simplicity and self-denial in the prophets' diets serves as a valuable lesson in prioritizing spiritual growth and contentment over material abundance.
- **Symbolic Acts**: Understanding the symbolic nature of the prophets' dietary practices helps modern readers appreciate the deeper spiritual meanings and lessons conveyed through these acts.

C. Final Thoughts on the Spiritual Lessons Drawn from Biblical Dietary Practices:

- **Holistic View of Nourishment**: Biblical dietary practices highlight the importance of holistic nourishment, encompassing physical, spiritual, and emotional well-being.
- **Unity and Respect**: The teachings of Jesus and Paul on dietary practices emphasize the importance of unity, respect, and love within the faith community. Believers are encouraged to prioritize relationships and the spiritual well-being of others over rigid adherence to dietary laws.

- **Ongoing Relevance:** While the specific dietary practices of the prophets may not be directly applicable today, the underlying principles of faith, obedience, simplicity, and commitment remain relevant and can guide believers in their spiritual journey.

In conclusion, the diets and lifestyles of Biblical prophets offer rich lessons in faith, obedience, and spiritual growth.

By examining these practices, you can gain insights into how to deepen your reliance on God, live simply, and nurture a spirit of commitment and unity within your communities.

References:

https://saltsandwest.com/blogs/news/the-healing-properties-of-linen-clothing#:~:text=Each%20fabric%20gives%20of%20a,bring%20you%20to%20a%200

AUDREA V. HEARD

ABOUT THE AUTHOR

AUDREA V. HEARD

Is the CEO of Power To Wealth Enterprises, Inc., Inspired By God (IBG) Publications, Inc., Scribby Fun, Inc. & Audrea V. Heard Enterprises, LLC.

Audrea answered the call on her life to preach the Gospel of Jesus Christ in 1998 and has been on FIRE for the Lord ever since. She is anointed by God to set people free from grief and depression, stemming from the loss of a loved one.

Apostle Audrea V. Heard-Abraham is an apostle to the nations, hailing from Eket, Akwa Ibom state in the country of Nigeria. She is an author of 20+ books and a serial entrepreneur. She is co-pastor with her husband, Sr. Apostle Nabaham Abraham of Miracle Of The Lord House Global Churches. Together they have four sons and many spiritual children in the Lord.

She is a full-time minister and business owner.

OTHER BOOKS BY THE AUTHOR

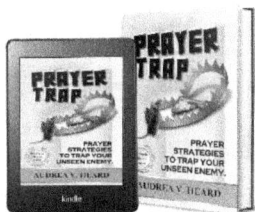

A strange thing happened in the life of Author Audrea V. Heard. While living in a rented house in Jacksonville, FL (in an urban area), she learned that the house was infested with rodents. She had to shake her fears and do something about it!

Initially terrified, she learned that she needed to man up because the rats would take over her home if she didn't. It was during this challenging season that she learned to not just trap the rats but trap the enemy and his tactic: FEAR.

What is his tactic in *your* life? Fear? Abandonment? Rejection? Whatever it is, 'Prayer Trap' will show you how to set a trap for the enemy, and reverse the tactics designed to kill your destiny.

Available at
amazon.com

AUDREA V. HEARD

Spirit Wives of the B.O.C. (Body of Christ) is a poignant journey for single women and women married to the wrong man.

Audrea's passion for writing this book comes from years of becoming a Spirit Wife many times over, but never chosen to be the wife of her God ordained mate! She gives a heart-to-heart talk with women about the pitfalls of singlehood in the church, becoming the legal wife to the wrong man and how the Super-Wonder-Wife Syndrome plagues 'Spiritual Women.'

She explores spiritual checkpoints like: the Spirit Wife's checklist, deadly reminiscing, breaking demonic forces & watching what you eat!

Available at
amazon.com

Take a journey for 90 days through the scriptures with these 3-part devotional series. Along your journey, you will be encouraged, overcome challenges, and receive your breakthrough!

You will document your journey and visit scriptures daily as you live the way God intended through His word. You will experience thought provoking moments, be enlightened, but challenged to grow and move forward into victorious, triumphant living!

Available at
amazon.com

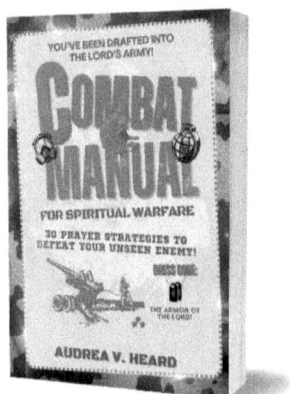

Get ready for 30 days of strategy to defeat the enemy in EVERY area of life. This strategic battle plan outlines your enemy's tactics with guided prompts to overcome these attacks. You will be enlightened, and strengthened while fortifying your spiritual armor during intense engagement with the enemy.

Grab this manual, head to your prayer closet and the enemy of your soul will be defeated in 30 days or less!

Lyrical Promises is a collection of poems, prayers and words of encouragement from our Father, God. Audrea began writing these poems in the year 1998 as a form of therapy, now she is excited to release them as a published work! Allow God to take you on a journey of hope, healing and understanding for His purpose over your life!

Available at
amazon.com

'Through the Fire' is the shattering but ultimately healing story of how Audrea recovered from the death of her 20 month old son and grandmother after a fire broke out in her house. Panicked, Audrea ran from the house but was unable to go back inside and save her family. Shockingly blamed for their deaths and fighting a lawsuit from her son's father, Audrea felt a sense of hopelessness; her life was falling apart with no end in sight. As she moved through the stages of grief and blame, she eventually found a deep stronghold of faith. God, she discovered, had a reason for everything, and through Him, peace and grace could be available. Moving and insightful, Through the Fire is for anyone struggling with grief.

CONTACT THE AUTHOR

You can find Audrea online by visiting her website:

WWW.AudreaVHeard.Com

To book Audrea for your next event:

✉ **info@audreavheard.com**

You can follow Audrea on social media:

@AuthorAudreaHeard

AUDREA V. HEARD

www.ingramcontent.com/pod-product-compliance
Lightning Source LLC
LaVergne TN
LVHW052031080426
835513LV00018B/2279